JOHANN SEBASTI

CANTATA

Sehet, wir gehn hinauf gen Jerusalem
Come ye, our way is up to Jerusalem
for 4 Solo Voices, Chorus and Chamber Orchestra
für 4 Solostimmen, Chor und Kammerorchester
BWV 159

Edited by / Herausgegeben von
Hans Grischkat

Ernst Eulenburg Ltd

London · Mainz · Madrid · New York · Paris · Tokyo · Toronto · Zürich

Inhalt

English translation by Henry S. Drinker

© 1960 Ernst Eulenburg & Co GmbH

All rights reserved.
No part of this publication may be reproduced, stored in a retrieval system,
or transmitted in any form or by any means,
electronic, mechanical, photocopying, recording or otherwise,
without the prior written permission of the publisher:

Ernst Eulenburg Ltd
48 Great Marlborough Street
London W1V 2BN

J. S. BACH, KANTATE Nr. 159:

«Sehet, wir gehn hinauf gen Jerusalem»

Die Kantate «Sehet, wir gehn hinauf gen Jerusalem» gehört zu den bekanntesten und meistaufgeführten Solo-Kantaten Bachs. Das Werk wurde wahrscheinlich zum Sonntag Estomihi 1729 geschrieben, entstand also gleichzeitig mit der Matthäus-Passion. So weisen auch fast alle Bach-Biographen auf die innere Verwandtschaft dieses Stückes mit der Passion hin. Wie zur Matthäus-Passion lieferte Picander auch zur vorliegenden Kantate den Text. Bach entnahm ihn der im Jahre 1728 in Leipzig veröffentlichten Sammlung «Cantaten Auf die Sonn- und Fest-Tage durch das gantze Jahr». In seinem Vorwort weist der Textdichter ausdrücklich auf seine Zusammenarbeit mit Bach hin: «Ich habe solches Vorhaben desto lieber unternommen, weil ich mir schmeicheln darf, daß vielleicht der Mangel der poetischen Anmut durch die Lieblichkeit des unvergleichlichen Herrn Capell-Meisters, Bach, dürfte ersetzet, und diese Lieder in den Haupt-Kirchen des andächtigen Leipzigs angestimmet werden.»

Das Herzstück der Kantate ist die unvergleichliche Baß-Arie «Es ist vollbracht». Ueber leisen Streicher-Akkorden duettiert die Singstimme mit der Oboe. Und es gehört zu den ergreifendsten Stellen in Bachschen Arien, wenn die Oboe immer wieder wie überschwenglich und mit stärkstem Ausdruck das Thema des Baß-Solisten aufgreift und dabei die den Instrumenten nun einmal auferlegte Fessel der Wortlosigkeit gleichsam abstreift und sprechend wird. Als Einleitungsstück der Kantate steht ein Zwiegespräch zwischen Christus und der Seele. Bach hat eigentümlicherweise die Christus-Worte aus dem Eingang des Sonntags-Evangeliums (Lukas 18, 31) «Sehet, wir gehn hinauf gen Jerusalem» als einfaches, nur vom Generalbaß begleitetes Arioso gesetzt, während die immer wieder dazwischengeschobenen Rezitativworte der Seele vom Streichorchester begleitet werden. Dabei ist den Christus-Worten im Continuo ein hartnäckig immer wiederkehrendes, in Tonleiterschritten um eine Quinte steigendes und dann plötzlich um eine Sept abstürzendes Motiv beigegeben, das mit seltener Prägnanz das Unentrinnbare des Leidensweges Christi symbolisiert. An dieses Einleitungsstück schließt sich eine schlichte Alt-Arie «Ich folge dir nach», zu der der Chor-Sopran mit Oboe aus dem Passions-Choral «O Haupt voll Blut und Wunden» die sechste Strophe «Ich will hier bei dir stehen» singt.

Die Kantate wurde erstmalig im Jahre 1886 von Ernst Naumann in Band 32 der Gesamtausgabe der Bachgesellschaft veröffentlicht. In der Neuen Bachausgabe liegt sie bis jetzt noch nicht vor. Leider gingen die Original-Partitur und -Stimmen verloren, so daß mir, ebenso wie dem Herausgeber der Bachausgabe, nur eine, wohl in den Jahren zwischen 1755 und 1770 entstandene Partiturabschrift und ein vollständiger Stimmensatz von Christian Friedrich Penzel als Druckvorlage zur Verfügung standen. Penzel war unter Bachs Nachfolger Harrer Präfekt des Thomanerchores und nach Harrers Tod auch kurze Zeit interimistisch dessen musikalischer Leiter gewesen. Das Penzelsche Material aus dem Besitz der ehemaligen Preußischen Staatsbibliothek (P 1048 und ST 633) befindet sich zur Zeit in treuhänderischer Verwahrung in der Westdeutschen Bibliothek Marburg. Der Marburger Bibliothek sei auch an dieser Stelle für ihre Unterstützung bei der Benutzung der Handschriften Dank gesagt.

Die Handschriften enthalten an vielen Stellen, vor allem in der Bezifferung der Arien Nr. 2 und 4, zweifellos viele Fehler oder zumindest zahlreiche zweifelhafte Stellen. Darum ist Naumann in der Alten Bachausgabe oft von der Vorlage abgewichen. Leider sind diese Abweichungen nicht konsequent kenntlich gemacht. Da er einen Teil seiner Aenderungen durch Klammern kennzeichnet, darf der Benutzer annehmen, daß die nicht in Klammern gesetzten Bezifferungen mit der Vorlage übereinstimmen. Doch ist dies nicht der Fall; mehr als die Hälfte der Aenderungen sind in keiner Weise kenntlich gemacht.

Einen Teil der Verbesserungs-Vorschläge der Alten Bachausgabe habe ich in diese Taschenpartitur übernommen, habe jedoch alle Abweichungen von der Penzelschen Abschrift durch Klammern oder Erwähnung am Schluß dieses Vorworts gekennzeichnet. Ueber einzelne Stellen sei im folgenden noch berichtet:

In der Arie Nr. 2, Takt 16 und 17, habe ich die eigentümliche Bezifferung der Vorlagen, die Naumann in die Alte Bachausgabe nicht aufgenommen hatte, belassen.

In derselben Arie steht abweichend von der üblichen Lesart in allen Vorlagen als vierte Choralzeile «bis dir dein Herze bricht» statt «wenn dir dein Herze bricht».

Im Rezitativ Nr. 3, Takt 3 heißt die vierte Note der Singstimme in allen Vorlagen d. Naumann ändert in der Alten Bachausgabe diese Note, die mit der Bezifferung unvereinbar scheint, in c. Ich habe diese Aenderung nicht übernommen, da mir trotz der klanglichen Härte der Stelle das d aus melodischen Gründen wahrscheinlicher zu sein scheint.

In der Arie Nr. 4, Takt 30 steht in allen Vorlagen als zweite Note der Violine II ein c. Naumann verbesserte diesen offensichtlichen Schreibfehler in der Alten Bachausgabe, indem er das c durch ein b ersetzte, während ich in der vorliegenden Taschenpartitur nach der Parallelstelle in Takt 7 ein d gesetzt habe.

Im selben Takt bringen die Vorlagen die letzten beiden Noten der Violine I als Viertel-Noten. Naumann nimmt auch hier einen Schreibfehler an und ändert nach der Parallelstelle Takt 7 in ♩. ♪. Die Aenderung wurde von mir in diese Ausgabe nicht übernommen.

Folgende offensichtliche Schreibfehler in der Bezifferung der Vorlage seien noch besonders erwähnt:

Nr. 1, Takt 7, (7) bei erster statt bei zweiter Note.

Takt 15, drittes Viertel fälschlich 6.

Takt 21, drittes Viertel fälschlich 6 statt $\cancel{6}$

Nr. 2, Takt 15, erste Note fälschlich $\frac{3}{4}$ statt $\frac{6}{5}$

Takt 22, erste Note 5 statt 6.

Takt 43, erste Note 5 statt 6.

Takt 79, zweites und drittes Achtel 4♮ 6.

Nr. 4, Takt 10, zweites Viertel 5 statt 4.

Takt 28, erstes und zweites Viertel 9 8 statt 8 7.

Takt 29, drittes und viertes Viertel 6- statt $\cancel{5}$ 6.

Takt 41, drittes Viertel $\cancel{2}$ statt $\cancel{\flat}$

Ueber die Mitwirkung des Fagotts ist in der Partiturvorlage kein Hinweis zu finden. Doch könnte man nach den Stimmen annehmen, daß sogar zwei Fagotte den Continuo in der Arie Nr. 2 mitspielen sollten; denn auf der Rückseite der beiden Violinstimmen ist unter der Ueberschrift «Fagotto» die Continuo-Stimme dieser Arie eingetragen.

Hans Grischkat.

Allgemeines zur Editionstechnik der Bach-Kantaten

Bei den vorliegenden Taschenpartituren handelt es sich um eine Veröffentlichung für die Praxis, nicht um eine wissenschaftliche Ausgabe. Darum werden die Chorstimmen im Violin- bzw. oktavierenden Violin- und Baß-Schlüssel notiert. Verschiedenheiten der äußeren Schreibform (♫♩♫ neben ♫♩ u. ä.) werden, ohne im einzelnen darüber zu berichten, vereinheitlicht.

Artikulationsbögen und Verzierungen, die aus Analogiegründen gesetzt werden sollten, werden in Klammern hinzugefügt.

Die Versetzungszeichen (♯ ♭ ♮) werden — auch bei der Generalbaß-Bezifferung — nach heutigem Brauch verwendet. Lediglich die Wiederholung eines in einem Takt mehrmals vorkommenden Versetzungszeichens wird, da auch für die Praxis ratsam, vielfach übernommen.

Bei der Wiedergabe der Texte wird die heutige Rechtschreibung gewählt, daneben aber weitgehend auf die Beibehaltung alter Wort- und Lautformen geachtet (stunden—bunden—kömmt—versammlet—Hülfe—darzu).

Textwiederholungen, die Bach häufig nur durch das Zeichen ✗ andeutete, werden ausgeschrieben.   H. G.

J. S. BACH: CANTATA No. 159:

«Come ye, our way is up to Jerusalem»

Amongst Bach's solo cantatas, «Behold, we go up to Jerusalem!» is not only one of the best known, but also one of the most frequently performed cantatas. Presumably he composed the work for the Sunday Estomihi of 1729, the period at which he was also working on the St. Matthew Passion. The text, which Bach selected from the collection «Cantatas for the Sun- and Holidays throughout the Whole Year» (published in Leipzig in 1728) was arranged by Picander, who had also supplied him with the text for the St. Matthew Passion. In his foreword, Picander specifically stresses his collaboration with Bach: «This task I have undertaken with all the more pleasure as I can flatter myself that perhaps the deficiencies of my poetic labours will be compensated for by the melodiousness of the incomparable Capell-Meister Bach, and that these hymns will be sung in the main churches by the devout people of Leipzig.»

The centre piece of the cantata is the glorious bass aria «His work is done». Supported by soft string chords, voice and oboe sing their duet, and it is one of the most impassioned moments in all of Bach's arias when the oboe, soaring with intense emotion, takes over the theme of the solo bass — it seems as if the bondage of wordlessness imposed on the instrument is broken, as if the oboe had gained the gift of coherent speech. — The cantata opens with a dialogue between Christ and the soul. Strangely enough Bach hat set the words of Christ at the beginning of the Sunday gospel (Luke 18, 31) «Behold, we go up to Jerusalem!» as a simple *Arioso,* accompanied only by the *basso continuo,* whereas the *recitativo*-words of the soul, with which the *arioso* is interspersed, are accompanied by the string orchestra. In addition to this, the *continuo* part underlining the words of Christ brings a stubbornly recurring motive — a rising scale through the interval of a fifth with a sudden drop of a seventh at the end — which symbolises with utmost intensity the inexorable course of Christ's passion. Linked to this introductory movement is a simple alto aria, «I follow Thee still», over which the chorus sopranos and the oboe sing the sixth verse «I stand beside Thee ever», of the passion chorale «O sacred head, sore wounded».

The cantata was first published in 1886 by Ernst Naumann in Vol. 32 of the Complete Edition of the Bach Society, and up to date it has not yet been re-issued in the New Bach Edition. The autograph score and parts unfortunately are lost, so that, like the editor of the Bach Society Edition, I only had a copy of the score and a complete set of parts by Christian Friedrich Penzel (probably dating from 1755 and 1770) at my disposal as a basis for this score. Under Bach's successor Harrer, Penzel was the prefect of the St. Thomas Choir, and after Harrer's death he took over as its acting musical director for a short period. The Penzel material, which is the property of the former Prussian State Library (P 1048 and ST 633) is at present in the keeping of the West German Library in Marburg, and at this point I wish to proffer my thanks to the Marburg library for their support and assistance in making these manuscripts available.

The manuscripts contain many mistakes or at least numerous doubtful points, especially in the bass figuration of the Arias Nos. 2 and 4, and for this reason Naumann in the Old Bach Edition often deviated from the manuscripts. Unfortunately these deviations have not been marked in a consistent manner: As some of his alterations have been placed in brackets, one would assume unbracketed bass figures to be in accordance with the manuscripts — however, more than half his alterations are devoid of any indication whatsoever.

This score contains some of the corrections suggested in the Old Bach Edition, but all deviations from Penzel's manuscripts are either placed in brackets or specially mentioned at the end of this foreword. The following points deserve individual mention:—

In *Aria No. 2*, bars 16—17, I have retained the somewhat strange bass figuration, which Naumann omits in the Old Bach Edition.

In this same aria, the German text of the fourth line of the chorale reads «*bis dir dein Herze bricht*» in all the manuscript parts, thereby deviating from the customary version «*wenn dir dein Herze bricht*».

In *Recitativo No. 3*, bar 3, the fourth note of the vocal line reads D in the manuscript. In the Old Bach Edition Naumann alters this note to C, as the D appears incompatible with the bass figuration. This alteration has not been incorporated into this edition, as despite the harmonic harshness the D appears to me to be correct for melodic reasons.

In *Aria No. 4*, bar 30, the manuscripts give a C for the second note in the Violin II part. Naumann, in the Old Bach Edition, altered this obviously erroneous C to B-flat, whereas in this present miniature score, in accordance with the parallel passage in bar 7, I have replaced the C by a D.

In the same bar the last two notes in the Violin I part are marked as crotchets in the manuscripts. Naumann assumes this too to be a mistake and alters them into a dotted crotchet followed by a quaver, so as to make them tally with the parallel passage in bar 7. This alteration was not incorporated into the present edition.

Furthermore mention must be made of the following obvious copyist's errors in the bass figurations of the manuscripts:

No. 1, bar 7: (7) on the first instead of on the second note.

      bar 15: third crotchet wrongly marked 6.

      bar 21: third crotchet wrongly marked 6 instead of $\cancel{6}$

No. 2, bar 15: first note wrongly marked $\frac{5}{4}$ instead of $\frac{6}{5}$

      bar 22: first note 5 instead of 6.

      bar 43: first note 5 instead of 6.

      bar 79: second and third quaver 4♮ 6.

No. 4, bar 10: second crotchet 5 instead of 4.

      bar 28: first and second crotchet 9 8 instead of 8 7.

      bar 29: third and fourth crotchet 6 — instead of ♯ 6

      bar 41: third crotchet $\frac{\cancel{6}}{2}$ instead of $\frac{\cancel{6}}{♭}$

No mention is made in the manuscript score regarding bassoons. However, judging by the parts one could assume that two bassoons were intended to play the *continuo* of the aria No. 2, for the *continuo* part of this aria, headed «Fagotto», is inscribed on the back of the two violin parts.

Hans Grischkat.

General remarks on the revision of the Bach Cantatas.

These present miniature scores are designed for practical use and are not a musicological edition. For this reason all vocal parts are printed in the treble and bass clef, or in the treble clef at the octave.

External differences of notation ⟨ ♪♩ ♪♩ for ♩♪♩♪ and similar instances⟩ are treated in uniform manner without detailed comment.

Phrasing marks and ornaments, when necessary by reason of analogy, are added in brackets.

Accidentals ⟨ ♯ ♭ ♮ ⟩ are placed in accordance with present day usage. Repetitions of recurring accidentals within the same bar, however, are frequently adhered to, as this is also advisable for practical reasons.

The German texts are reproduced in modern spelling, but much attention is given to the retention of old forms of words and vowels.

Repetitions in the text, which Bach often merely indicated by the sign ℀, are printed in full.

Hans Grischkat

Sehet, wir gehn hinauf gen Jerusalem

Dominica Estomihi

1. (Arioso und Rezitativ)

1) So in Stimme; in Partitur: as

No. 1056   EE 6161   © 1960 Ernst Eulenburg & Co GmbH

nach Je – ru – sa – lem, ach, lei – der in die Höl – le ge – hen!
my Je – ru – sa – lem, yea, ev – ver deep in Hell will lan – guish.

2. Duetto (Arie mit Choral)

Soprano
Oboe

Alto

Continuo
(Fagott) [1]

Ich fol – – ge dir
I fol – – low Thee
piano

Ich
I

nach, ich fol – – – – ge dir nach
still, I fol – – – – low Thee still

1) s. Vorwort

1) So in Partitur und Fagottstimme; in Continuostimmen: h

1) So in bezifferter Orgelstimme; in Partitur und den anderen Stimmen eine Terz tiefer: es

1) Im Original: den Gift

4. Aria Basso solo

Es ist_ voll-bracht, es ist_ voll-bracht, das Leid

His work is_ done, the bat-tle_ won, the pain_____

1) So in Stimme; in Partitur: g - fis

16

Nacht _____ !
well _____ !

Es ist __ voll - bracht, es ist __ voll -
His work is done, the bat - tle

bracht!
won!

18